D1256842

Sea Cows Don't Moo!

By Susan Blackaby

School Specialty. Publishing

Text Copyright © 2007 School Specialty Publishing. Manatee Character © 2003 by John Lithgow. Manatee Illustration © 2003 by Ard Hoyt.

Send all inquiries to:
School Specialty Publishing
8720 Orion Place
Columbus, OH 43240-2111

ISBN 0-7696-4243-8

1 2 3 4 5 6 7 8 9 10 PHXBK 12 11 10 09 08 07 06

Table of Contents

Look at Me!

Look under the water.
Do you see a large gray animal?
Is it swimming slowly?
Does it have a wrinkled face?
Does it have whiskers on its snout?
Does it have a tail shaped like a paddle?
Then, it must be a manatee like me!

Manatee Mentions

Christopher Columbus saw a manatee when he sailed to the New World. He thought it was a mermaid!

Manatee Senses

Manatees use their senses
just like you do.
Their eyes see well in murky water.
Their ears hear low tones.
Manatees use their sense of touch, too.
They use their lips to feel things
that are nearby.
They use their bodies to feel things
around them.

Manatee Mentions

Manatees have long whiskers on their faces and tiny hairs on their bodies. The hairs help the manatee sense changes in the water around it.

Size Me Up!

Manatees are king-sized creatures.
Some are very big.
They can be 13 feet long,
over twice as long as a person.
Some are very heavy.
They can weigh 3,500 pounds.
How big is an average manatee?
It is about the size of a small car!

Manatee Mentions

Though the manatee is called a "sea cow," it is related to the elephant.

Coming Up for Air

Manatees are like other marine mammals.
They cannot breathe under water.
They must come out of the water to breathe air.
When resting, manatees can stay under the water for 20 minutes.
When eating, manatees must come up for air every few minutes.
When swimming, they need to breathe more often.

Manatee Mentions

Manatees breathe through their noses. They poke them up out of the water to get air.

Manatee Homes

Manatees like warm, shallow water.
They live near coasts.
They live in **estuaries**.
They live in bays and swamps.
Manatees in the United States spend
the winter in Florida.
In the summer, they **migrate**.
They travel north to Georgia.
They travel west to Alabama.

Manatee Mentions

Manatees can live in a saltwater or freshwater **habitat**.

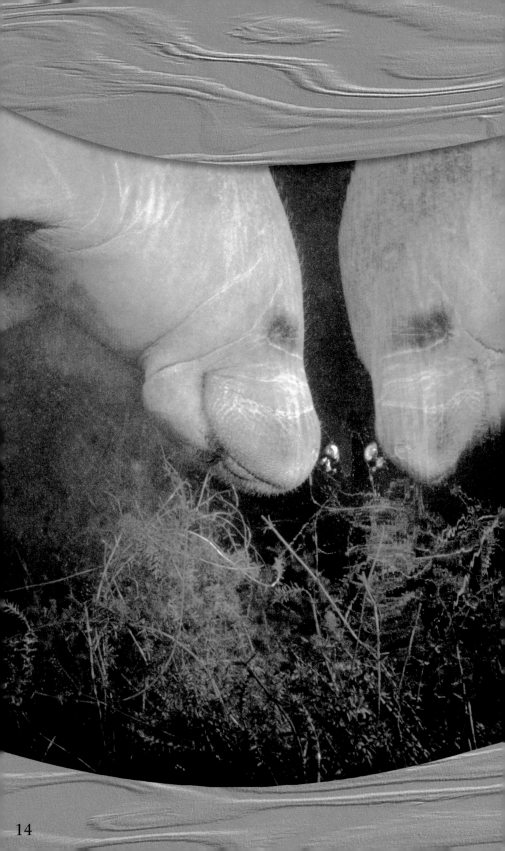

Manatee Menu

Manatees eat only plants.
They use their **flippers** and lips
to grab food.
They eat grasses.
They eat **mangrove** leaves.
They eat floating plants.
Manatees eat about 70 pounds
of plants a day.

Manatee Mentions

Manatees do not have front teeth. They have big, flat
molars. When a molar wears down, a new one takes
its place.

Manatee Mothers

A baby manatee is a **calf**.
A manatee gives birth to one calf
every three years.
Calves are born in spring or summer.
A calf stays close to its mother
for two years.
The mother shows the calf what to eat.
She shows it how to find warm water
during cool months.

Manatee Mentions

A mother manatee uses **vocalization** to speak to her
calf. She chirps and squeaks. Her calf hears her. It
chirps and squeaks back to her.

Manatee Activities

Manatees are peaceful.
They do not fight.
Manatees play together.
They share their seaside home
with other animals.

Manatee Mentions
Manatees have been known to surf waves while playing!

Manatees move slowly.
They spend a lot of time eating.
They can eat for six hours a day.
They also spend a lot of time sleeping.
They can sleep for 12 hours a day.
The rest of the time, manatees swim.
They explore the underwater world.

Manatee Mentions

Manatees do not dive deep in the water. They stay close to the surface where the water is warm.

Saving the Manatee

Manatees are an **endangered species**.
What dangers do manatees face?
Crocodiles eat newborn calves.
So do sharks and alligators.
Scientists think manatees can live
a long time.
Without threats, they may live for 60
years or more.

Manatee Mentions

Snooty is a famous manatee. He lives at the Parker
Manatee Aquarium in Florida. He is over 50 years old!

People are a danger to manatees, too.
People take over seaside habitats.
They build homes near the beach.
People fill in swamps with dirt
to make new land for houses.
People **pollute** rivers.
These actions hurt manatees
and their homes.

Manatee Mentions

There may be only 2,000 Florida manatees left in the United States today.

More homes near the beach mean more people.

Many of these people have boats.

People in boats run over manatees by accident.

Manatees cannot swim fast enough to get out of the way.

Many people also fish.

Manatees can get tangled in fishing nets and lines.

Manatee Mentions

Sea World® in Orlando, Florida, has a program that rescues and cares for sick and injured manatees. They are returned to their natural habitat when well.

People are working together to save the manatee.

National laws protect all marine mammals.

State laws protect coastal habitats where manatees live.

Local laws set boating speed limits. If boaters slow down, they run over fewer manatees.

Manatee Mentions

The "Save the Manatee® Club" started in Florida in 1981. Its goal is to keep the manatee from disappearing from the earth.

Vocabulary

calf–a baby manatee. *The manatee calf swims with its mother.*

endangered–in danger of becoming extinct. *The manatee is an endangered animal.*

estuary–a place where a river meets the ocean. *The manatee swims in the estuary.*

flipper–a broad, flat limb used for swimming. *The manatee uses its flipper to steer.*

habitat–a place where an animal or a plant naturally grows and lives. *Some manatees live in a saltwater habitat.*

mangrove–a tropical evergreen tree or shrub with lots of branches and roots that look like trunks. *The mangrove grows in a swamp.*

migrate–to move from place to place with the seasons. *Manatees migrate from place to place in search of warm water.*

molar–a tooth with a flat surface for grinding. *Manatees use their molars to chew plants.*

pollute–to make dirty. *Waste water can pollute rivers.*

species–a group of animals or plants that are the same kind. *A manatee is a species of mammal.*

surf–to ride on the crest of a wave. *Manatees surf the waves with their bodies.*

vocalization–to use the voice to make sounds. *Manatees use vocalization to communicate with one another.*

Think About It!

1. What do manatees eat? How much food do they eat each day?

2. How are manatees like other marine mammals?

3. How does a mother manatee care for her calf?

4. Why do you think manatees are called "sea cows"?

5. What do people do that harms the manatee? What are people doing to save the manatee?

The Story and You!

1. If you ate only vegetables, what would you have for lunch?

2. When you swim under the water, how are you like a manatee? How are you different from a manatee?

3. How does your mother use vocalization to communicate with you?

4. Do you think it would be fun to have a manatee for a pet? How would you care for the manatee?

5. If you wanted to make a bumper sticker about helping manatees, what would it say?